WALKS IN SUSSEX

Walks in Sussex

NORMAN WILLIS

SPURBOOKS LIMITED

Published by
SPURBOOKS LIMITED
6 Parade Court
Bourne End
Buckinghamshire

ISBN 0 904978 80 X

At the time of publication all the walks in this book were along paths designated as official footpaths, but it should be borne in mind that deviation orders may be made from time to time.

Printed by Maund & Irvine, Tring, Herts.

Contents

Introduction

I was very happy to accept the proposal that I should compile this book of walks in Sussex, but I must admit to doing so with a certain amount of trepidation. Having at that time just completed a walking route across Surrey and Sussex to connect the North Downs with the South Downs, I was well aware of the problems concerning footpaths throughout Sussex.

Much of the usual lattice-work of footpaths and bridleways has disappeared through a variety of reasons. Some paths have been ploughed up, fenced off or marked 'private' while others have not been used for some time and have become too overgrown to walk. This made it very difficult to plan round walks, and in some cases it has been necessary to use short stretches of quiet country road to connect existing paths.

The end product is contained within these pages and the walks will take you through the different types of countryside that make up the County of Sussex. To obtain maximum enjoyment, each should be walked during the four seasons of the year as rambling should never be considered as an activity confined solely to the spring and summer. The autumn scene is magnificent when the leaves have turned colour and a tramp across the fields in the winter will show you many things previously hidden by foliage, as well as giving you rosy cheeks.

Fresh air and exercise make you hungry and picnics make a nice break in the day. If this is your first experience of rambling, you will find a small haversack useful for carrying your lunch and raingear, thus leaving your arms free. Of prime importance is a pair of strong shoes. Even after a dry spell you will often find mud lingering under the trees, and wet feet are not particularly conducive to the enjoyment of a country walk.

Where possible, I have included bus routes to the starting points, but it is always wise to check these, as route numbers and running times are subject to change at short notice.

In this book you will find reference to Hilaire Belloc, the writer and poet who loved Sussex very much. His book called 'The Four Men', is a description of a walk through the county in 1902. By coincidence, some of my walks parallel his, and you may find it interesting to obtain a copy for comparison. He lived in Shipley until his death in 1953 and Walk 9 includes a visit to his house and windmill.

Now it only remains for me to remind you to obey the 'Country Code'.

Happy Walking:
NORMAN WILLIS

Abbreviations: FP—Footpath; SP—Signpost.

WALK 1

ST. LEONARDS FOREST, COLGATE.

5½ miles.

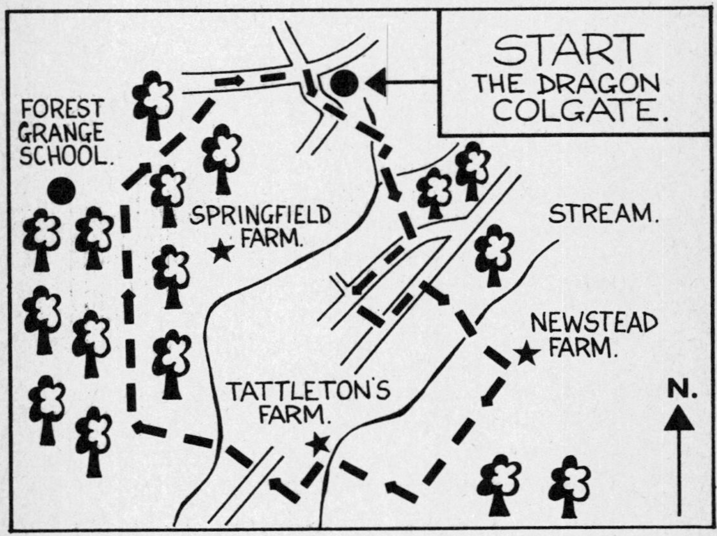

The forest is named after St. Leonard who is said to have slain a dragon living there. In the 17th century it was described as an evil and unwholesome place but happily it is now a pleasant mixture of woods and farmland with numerous streams and rivers finding their way into ponds and lakes.

By car: Colgate is 2 miles west of Pease Pottage at the end of the M23 (Junction 11) where it joins the A23. No car park, but you can find limited parking on the verge nearby or pull up into the edge of the woods. Do not use the pub car park without permission.

By bus: Tillingbourne Service 451 from Horsham. Weekdays only.

Take the lane at the side of *The Dragon* marked Private—No Through Road. Go past another sign *Dangerous Bend* and just before reaching a house called *Bisham,* double back sharp left. After a few yards, at a FP sign, turn right with a house and garden right and views across the valley left. Continue downhill with woods on both sides, cross a stream and keeping to the right of the pond make your way to a broad crossing track where you turn right. After a short distance turn left where the FP sign is nailed high up on a tree. Still in the woods, go downhill to cross a fast flowing stream before making your way uphill, ignoring tracks left and right, to a stile which you cross, and then turn left to a road. In the road, turn right and after about a quarter of a mile, at a sign on your right *To Spring Farm,* turn left along a path between hedges. On reaching a FP sign, continue through the gate and keeping to the left side of the field make your way to a stile on the far side.

Go over the stile into the road opposite a house called *Elenge Plat* and turn left. A short distance after passing *Lythmere House* right, turn right over a stile at a FP sign. Follow this path downhill into the valley crossing another stile before you reach the river running through the wood. Follow the path over the wooden bridge, through a metal gate and uphill keeping the gorse hedge on your immediate left. At the top of the hill, cross a broken stile. Go straight across **KEEPING TO THE LEFT HAND FENCE,** as this is where the right of way exists, and this brings you out onto the concrete path through a narrow gap left in the wooden fence. Here, turn right and follow the farm road for three quarters of a mile until you reach a kind of 'T' junction where the road turns sharp left. At this point turn right onto a bridleway (SP) and follow this through two metal gates, eventually going downhill at the right hand edge of a field to a wooden gate at the bottom. Go through the gate, and over a plank bridge, and follow the path through a wide gap in the hedge and down to a stream. Having crossed the narrow stone bridge, turn left through a wooden gate and follow the feint path half right across the field to another gate where you turn right along a path between fences.

On reaching the road, go straight over to cross a stile and continue along a clear path through the wood. Follow this path over a wide crossing track or fire break, and downhill to cross a wooden bridge over the river at the bottom of the valley.

Proceed uphill again, crossing another stile and ignoring any paths to left or right. Still making your way uphill, trees now close in and you may be tempted to think once more about St. Leonard's fight with the dragon. The story goes that the dragon inflicted many wounds on St. Leonard and wherever drops of his blood fell to the ground, Lilies of the Valley sprang up. Needless to say, in May of each year the flowers return to bear silent witness to the fortitude of St. Leonard.

Eventually you come out of the trees into a broad track where you turn left. After a few yards, at a 'T' junction, turn right along a very wide bridle path that stretches on between the woods for about a mile. This is an ideal picnic area and place for children to play as a break from continuous walking.

At the end of the mile, bear right with the path and straight on for nearly half a mile to some wooden gates. These gates allow you exit from within the boundaries of the Forestry Commission and you continue along a rough road to the main road where you turn right. Soon you will see the red sign of the *Dragon* public house where, with the right timing, you may slake your thirst.

WALK 2

WARNINGLID.

4 miles.

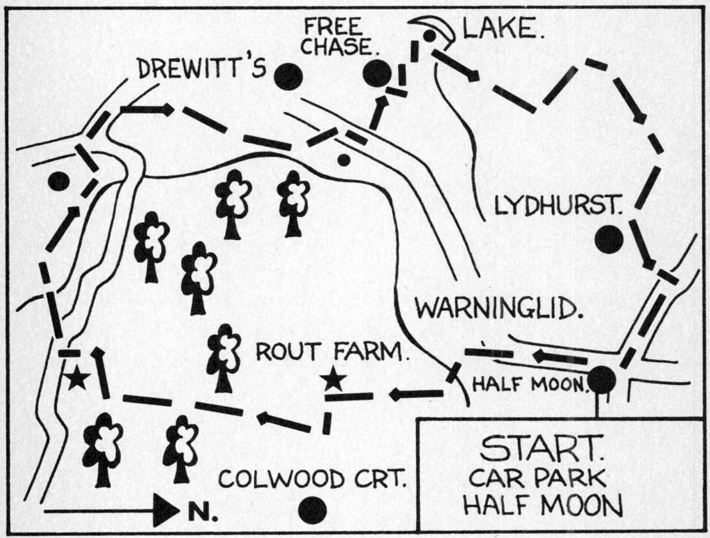

Warninglid is a small village approximately seven miles SE of Horsham. The walk is very pleasant with varied scenery taking you through farm country at first and then on to the woods of an immaculately kept estate.

By car: From the A23 Brighton Road, turn left onto the A279 (SP Cowfold) just before Handcross. At 'T' junction turn right. (SP Lewes and Newhaven) then bear right (SP Cowfold and Horsham A279). After about 2½ miles, turn left onto the B2115 (SP Haywards Heath and Warninglid). After two miles, at Warninglid crossroads, park in the car park of the *Half Moon* public house. The publicans have no objection to you using their car park while walking but would appreciate the courtesy of being told that your car is parked there.

By bus: Route 171—from Haywards Heath Bus Station to Warninglid *Half Moon;* Route 299—from Horsham to Warninglid Village and start at *Half Moon* Public House.

On leaving the car park turn left, soon passing the *Old Smithy* general stores and Post Office. Where the road bends sharp right at the *Rifleman* public house you continue straight on along the bridleway to the right of *Hillside Cottage.* Bear left with the road passing a timbered house and crossing a stream before going up hill on a concrete road towards a farm. On reaching the farm, turn left between a wooden fence and the first long grey building on your left. With the building now on your right, follow the fence round to the right until you reach a gate. Go through the gate and keep to the right hand edge of the field following the fence on your immediate right. On the far side of the field, go through a small wooden gate and continue ahead between wire fences with an orchard on your right.

Pass through another wooden gate and when you reach the farm at the bottom of the hill, go over the stile between two metal gates. Bear right to join the road that curves left and downhill past *Chapel Lodge* to meet the road at the 'T' junction. Turn right and where the road bears sharp right, go through a gateway to the left of the house sign *Chargrove.* Go straight on between the trees, cross a stile and then slightly up hill keeping to the fence on your right. At the top of the field, pass through a gap in the fence, go half right to the old iron water pump on the rise and then half left to the five-barred gate in the hedge opposite.

Follow the path between bushes and trees, soon bearing right at the top of the hill with the occasional glimpse of the view across the valley on your right. Eventually you pass to the side of a double tree trunk gateway and emerge from the trees into a road at the side of a private garden by a white house called *Ramatuelle.* Turn right and make your way down to the road. Cross the road and turn right to follow bridleway sign between *Bee House Cottage* right and houses on the left. This soon changes from a private road to a path through the woods.

After about half a mile, just after passing a large pink painted house left, you come out onto the road, where you turn right and almost immediately left along a drive opposite *Port Wood*

Cottage. The drive bears right, then left past a house and instead of going on to a very oddly-shaped building, turn right to the cross roads. Here you take the path opposite that bears left and downhill, then turns sharp right and on through a farmyard. When you reach the white fence barring your way to a lake, turn right, cross a wooden bridge and go through a metal gate. You then turn right along a FP that eventually takes you through a metal swing gate and a little farther on to a fork in the path by a FP signpost.

Ignore the intriguing path that goes off right uphill and take the left hand path, which is in fact straight on. When you come to a wooden swing gate, go through, then turn right and keep straight on ignoring the path to your left. Keep on going uphill through the woods eventually passing a FP with a swing gate on your right just before joining an asphalt road.

NOTE: The owner of this ground has made application to change the existing Right of Way. If approved, the path will swing to the left of the tennis court but will still emerge in the road where you turn right for Warninglid crossroads and the *Half Moon* pub.

To continue: Nearly a quarter of a mile after joining the made up road, you pass between a house right and tennis court left. On coming to a junction of paths, follow the FP sign that takes you straight on, with the flag pole left, to a metal gate. Go through this gate and on to a second gate that leads you into the B2115 where you turn right and keep straight on for the *Half Moon*.

WALK 3

HORSTED KEYNES

4 miles.

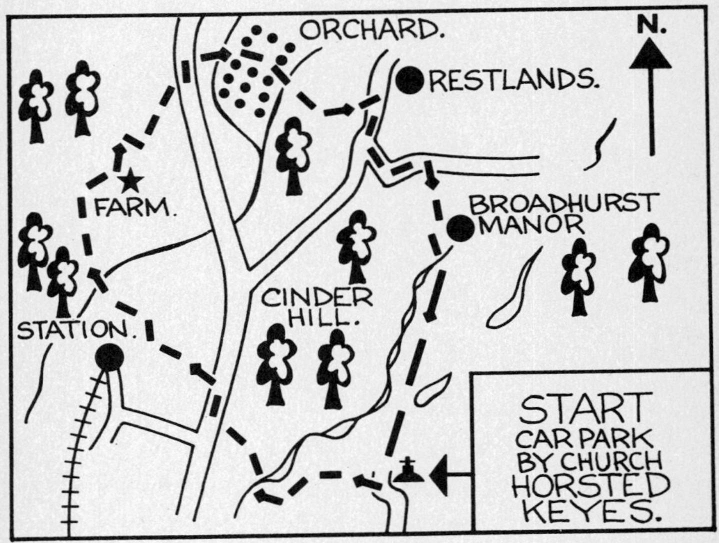

This really is a beautiful walk for any time of the year. Starting by a lake, it takes you through farmland, orchards, past an old Manor House and back along a bridlepath following a chain of small lakes.

By car: From East Grinstead, take the A22 south passing through Forest Row and approximately two miles further on turn right onto the A275. Continue for about 3 miles and just after passing a sign *Danehill* left, turn right SP Horsted Keynes. After a mile, turn left at a 'T' junction. Opposite the *Crown Garage* left, turn right along road marked '*To School and Church*'. At 'T' junction turn right and park your car in the small area adjacent to the church gate.

By bus: Southdown Bus—Service 170:
From (a) Brighton—Pool Valley
(b) Haywards Heath Bus Station
(c) East Grinstead Railway Station

Facing the church, take the rough road and bridleway to the left and just past *Old Church Cottage* and opposite the school (both right) turn left down a broad track. This soon bears left then right passing a timbered farm house with an unusual type of old iron water pump near the hedge.

A little further on, you catch sight of a lake on your right. Here you turn right over the steam and with the lake on your immediate right make your way toward the sound of rushing water. This is caused by a small weir that controls the water level and guides the over-flow beneath your feet to a river.

Continue to a double wooden gate and cross the stile. Follow the path at the left-hand edge of the field and just before it bears right by a double telegraph pole, turn left over a wood fence and ditch. Follow the clear path through the wood and on coming to a wide crossing track, turn left over a mound and then right to continue in your original direction. You emerge from the wood and cross a stile onto a strip of grass running across a ploughed field to another stile.

In the road, turn right for about 30 yards and then turn left over a stile. Keep to the left-hand edge of the field and in the far corner, go over a fence and continue along a narrow path between the wood left, and wire fence right. Cross a stile at the end of the path into an open field and turn half right (no FP visible) to the far corner where a gate leads you on to an old railway bridge.

To your left is Horsted Keynes station and to your right nothing except a notice claiming railway property where the lines have been removed by Mr. Beeching's axe!

Continue over the bridge and then turn right along the grass track between the bramble bushes and follow this to a wooden gate. Over the gate into a field where you turn right, pass through a gap in the fence by a tree and turn left keeping to the edge of the field making your way downhill to a bridge. Cross this combined bridge and fence and follow the feint path to a metal gate, that gives you access to a larger field with no visible path. From the gate go diagonally left to the opposite corner and cross the wire fence where at one time there used to be a stile.

Diagonally again, this time right and uphill to the farm where you pass through a wooden gate into the farmyard and turn left along the rough road. Bear right over another railway bridge, and immediately sharp left through a metal gate. Go straight ahead through a gap in the hedge and continue keeping to the feint track in line with the trees. To your left on a clear day, there is a fine view across the valley.

At the far side of the field, climb the wooden fence/gate to the right of the gap in the hedge and make your way towards the buildings ahead keeping the pond on your right. Pass through a gap in the buildings and turn right past the front of the house down to the road opposite an old timbered house called *Tanyard*.

Turn left and just past *Vaex End Cottage* go through a wooden gate on your right where a cement FP sign is marked with a yellow spot.

Once through the gate turn right, through another gateway also marked yellow and keeping to the centre of the field, go downhill to a gate that leads you on to the top of a small dam. Cross the top of the dam with a lake left and water-drop into the river on your right. On the opposite bank turn left then right following the yellow way marks to emerge from the wood at the edge of an orchard.

Here you need to be a little careful. Ignore the crossing track and go ahead into the orchard keeping between the trees with yellow spots (the spots are faded and not easy to see and there is no visible path). Continue as directed through the orchard and on the far side, where you look out onto an open field, turn left, then right, keeping to the right of an old caravan and nissen hut.

You are now walking downhill with another orchard on your left and the open field right. On reaching the wood at the bottom of the hill, turn right and after a few yards turn left through the wood (more yellow spots) and over a stile into a sizeable field. Turn left, and keeping to the edge of the field go straight on, then bearing right until eventually you reach a stile by a wooden gate. Cross the stile into a road where you turn right, soon turning left at the SP to Birchgrove and Chelwood Gate.

Just after the road bears left, turn right along the bridlepath to Horsted Keynes. This is more like a private road than a bridlepath and it takes you to an elegant gateway leading to the lovely old Broadhurst Manor House which unfortunately is not open to the public. Here you turn right onto a rough brick road and after a few yards, turn left through a gateway with an old house on your right.

Keep straight on along this rough road ignoring all paths left and right for about a mile. For the entire distance, you have the river on your right flowing through a number of small lakes with the occasional water-drop where the river has been dammed. Just after the river disappears from sight among the trees you come to the largest lake of all on your left. There are many superb spots for a picnic here but please make sure that you leave the area free from litter.

Continue straight on, eventually returning to and passing the school on your left and back to your car. If you came by bus, retrace your steps to the centre of Horsted Keynes.

WALK 4

WEIR WOOD RESERVOIR

3½ miles.

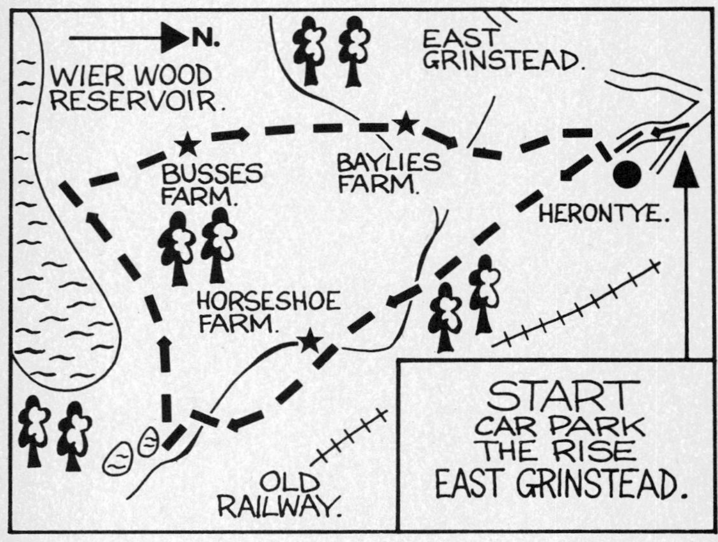

This is a pleasant walk through the fields south of East Grinstead to the Weir Wood Reservoir which is surrounded on all sides by gently sloping hills. Because the northern bank is fenced off, it has become something of a nature reserve for wild fowl and it is delightful to see the various species in the water mingling with the yachts from the club on the south bank. The return trip is made along a rough farm track connecting two farms.

By car: A22 to East Grinstead travelling south. Pass through Felbridge, and at East Grinstead after crossing the second railway bridge, continue through the main shopping centre uphill and turn sharp left. As you come level with the *Crown* public house, branch right passing to the right of the Midland Bank and take the second road on your right called *Hermitage Lane.* Just after a road on the right called *The Rise,* turn left and where the road forks at a white house with green gables, find a place to park your car.

Having parked the car, take the right fork along a rough road soon passing a house called *Blue Spindels* on your right. Turn sharp right with the road and just after an entrance to a housing estate with three concrete posts on your right, turn left over a stile. Go straight across the field (no FP visible) to cross a stile on the opposite side. After a few yards between fences, cross another stile left with the top bar painted white and cross the field diagonally left to a gap in the fence (white painted posts) where you cross a small bridge. Keeping the wooden fence on your immediate left, cross the field to another stile and footbridge that leads you out into an open field.

Continue straight ahead in line with but keeping to the left of the power lines until you reach the far left-hand corner of the field where you cross two more bridges and then up a narrow path between fences. On reaching the road, turn right through the white gates of *Horseshoe Farm* soon crossing two stiles (one broken) and then half left uphill to a third stile.

Cross the next area of cultivated land by way of the grass path left by the farmer and just after passing under two sets of power lines, turn right for a short distance, then turn left over a bridge and continue your original direction keeping the river on your immediate left.

The river zig-zags along until you reach a stile which you should ignore and instead turn right along the left hand edge of the field. Pass through a gap in the hedge and you are now walking with a wire fence and view of the reservoir pump-house on your left. To your right you can see the tower of East Grinstead church on the skyline.

As you reach the top of the hill so the reservoir comes into sight with the yacht club on the far side. At the top of the field, bear left through a broken wooden gate now walking along a narrow FP with views of the reservoir left and a wood right.

Keep to this path and notice the point where you pass under the pylon lines. A quarter of a mile further on from this point turn right over a kind of stile almost hidden by the bushes. To help you recognise the place, look out for three fading white paint blobs on the fence pillar opposite the stile.

Keep to the right hand edge of the field, on the far side, go through a metal gate to join the bridlepath. This leads you to the first farm and through the farmyard bearing right past the farmhouse.

Now walking along a rough farm road, with East Grinstead church tower in front of you, continue for about 1¾ miles passing through a second farmyard eventually returning to the stile on your right that acted as your starting point. From here, retrace your steps back to the car.

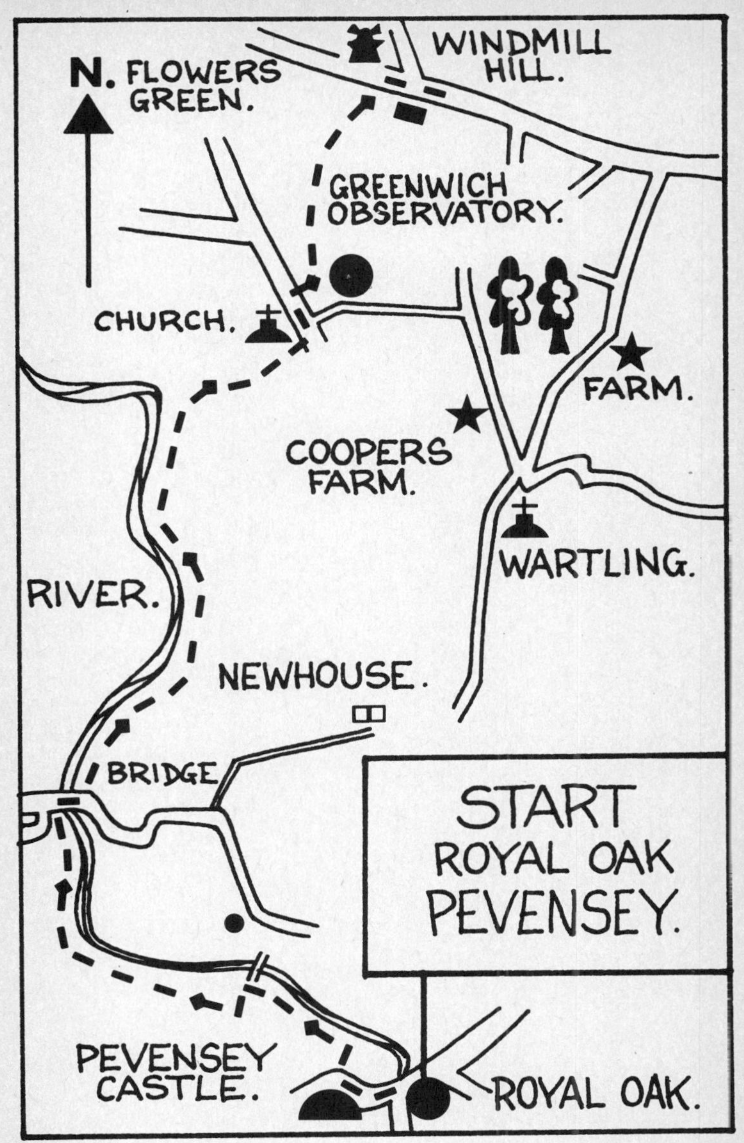
N.
FLOWERS GREEN.
WINDMILL HILL.
GREENWICH OBSERVATORY.
CHURCH.
FARM.
COOPERS FARM.
WARTLING.
RIVER.
NEWHOUSE.
BRIDGE
START
ROYAL OAK
PEVENSEY.
PEVENSEY CASTLE.
ROYAL OAK.

WALK 5

PEVENSEY TO WINDMILL HILL

6 miles.

This is one of the two A to B walks in the book and it takes you from Pevensey Castle to Windmill Hill near Herstmonceux via the Royal Greenwich Observatory at Herstmonceux Castle. The Observatory can be visited but it is wise to check opening times. For three-quarters of the distance you are walking beside a river that meanders its way across the area called Pevensey Levels. However, it is not as flat and uninteresting as the name would have you believe and there is plenty to interest the naturalist along the river banks.

By bus: No. 196 from Eastbourne to Pevensey Old Mint House, (opposite the *Royal Oak* public house). Return: No. 495 Windmill Hill Post Office to Eastbourne.

By car: A259 Eastbourne to Pevensey—park in the Castle car park. Not being a circular walk, it is necessary to arrange for someone to pick you up at the finish or drop you at the start, or you will have to re-trace your steps back to your car, thus doubling the distance.

Your starting point is the *Royal Oak* public house. Turn left towards the entrance of the castle but bear right with the road passing the *Priory Court Hotel* on your right. Pass the next house and immediately turn right down a slope between the side of the house and allotments.

Continue along the bridle path with the castle behind you, soon passing through a gate (with a stone footpath sign) to follow the feint track bearing right with the edge of the field. Go through a seven barred metal gate, cross a dyke, and on to the river bank where you turn left. Follow the river until you reach a barrier of bramble bushes where you must turn left for a short distance and then right over a stile. There is a worn sheep track that runs parallel to the river and leads you to a 'crossing point' in the barbed wire fence. Ignore this and turn right for a few yards to cross the fence at what used to be a stile. Ignore the metal bridge to your right and turn left to regain the sheep track. Sometimes splitting into several tracks, it eventually leads you to a muddy gully enclosed by trees and bushes. Cross the gully and the wire fence (no stile, again) and follow now an almost invisible path with the river still on your right.

On the far side of the field, pass between the wooden posts of an old gateway and continue as before. If you look back now, you can see two towers of Pevensey Castle on the skyline. The path eventually bears left a little to pass through a gap in the hedge and again you follow the track along the river bank to a wooden fence. Either climb the metal gate or pass through the smaller wooden gate to its left and make your way to a small stone bridge crossing a dyke. On the other side, the track becomes more visible as it bears left towards some farm buildings but you must stay on the river bank to pass through a small rough wooden gate to the left of a metal barred gate. Keep to the left of the pylon and in the far left hand corner of the field go through a small wooden gate. Cross the strip of farm enclosure, pass through a second gate and along a narrow 'right of way' to the road.

Here turn right, crossing a bridge with a sluice gate in the river on your left and at the 'T' junction with signpost *Hailsham* left and *Pevensey* right, turn right. Cross another bridge and pass through the second wooden gate on your left. From now on for about two miles, you keep to the river bank with the river on your left. On a clear day you can see the Observatory ahead of you moving around on the horizon as you follow the turns of the river. Pass through or over a series of gates as you progress along the bank and eventually you come to some gates bearing the request *Please Shut the Gate*. After passing through THREE of these, follow the directions carefully.

Go through another gate and you find that the river is now taking a long sweeping bend to the right, so that for a while you are heading towards a church in the distance. Pass a narrow wooden and metal bridge across the river and on reaching the next gate, do not go through but turn right keeping to the left hand edge of the field. When you come to a five barred wooden gate, turn left through it and continue along the grassy track with a ditch left and dyke right. Go through a metal gate to follow a farm track, first bearing left and then right with a square mesh fence left. Turn sharp left with the fence, now walking uphill. You can see the Observatory quite clearly just over to your right soon to disappear behind a big red building surrounded by masts.

Bear left with the track and to your left, on a clear day, you have a wonderful view of the Pevensey Flats. Your height may come as a surprise until you realise that over the last half mile you have been steadily climbing.

At the end of the track, go through the green metal gate into the farmyard passing through the yard and onto the road. Turn left with the church left and the entrance to the Royal Greenwich Observatory on your right. Keep straight on along the road and almost opposite a house on your left, you will see a small wooden gate with a footpath sign *To Windmill Hill.* This is the path you need for the last section of the walk and after passing through the corner of a fir tree plantation, another gate guides you onto a narrow footpath between overhanging trees. At the end of this tunnel of trees, make your way downhill keeping to the right hand edge of the field. Pass between two short wooden fences at the bottom of the hill and then the path takes you uphill again with the fence still on your right.

When you reach the far righthand corner of the field, turn right over a bent and twisted metal fence and immediately left through a wooden gate. Continue ahead, and then in quick succession, over first a fence and then a stile before the path takes you through a black metal gate, (which is frequently already open) and on to a rough made up road. Ignore footpath signs first right and then left and you will soon see on your left, about half a mile away, the remains of an old windmill without sails.

Follow the road between buildings to the main road (A271). Turn right passing the *Horseshoe Inn,* a large rambling timbered building which has become a restaurant and public house, and a little farther on opposite the *Windmill Hill Stores* is a bus stop and journey's end.

WALK 6

ASHURST CIRCULAR

3 miles.

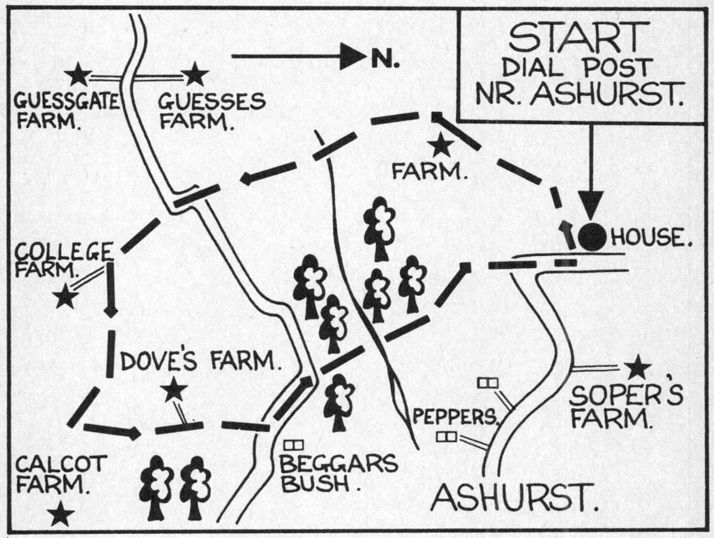

This walk starts at the Public Bridleway signpost just over 1 mile from the village of Ashurst. Ashurst is about 3½ miles north of the South Downs and as you ramble through woods and fields you are presented with tantalising glimpses of these guardians of the southcoast.

By car: Ashurst is on the B2135 which starts about 1 mile to the north of *Steyning* on the A283 and ends 1¾ miles north of Dial Post on the A24. On reaching *Ashurst* and the public house called *The Fountain* turn right if travelling south, or left if travelling north, to *Dial Post* as signposted. At the T junction turn right (to 12th-century church) and almost immediately turn left at signpost to *Dial Post*. About a mile further on you turn right on a hairpin bend (red postbox left) and 150 yards up the road you will see a house on your left with a bridleway sign pointing left. There is plenty of parking room on the grass verges.

Using the wooden Public Bridleway signpost as your starting point, head due west along the path passing the part timbered house on your right. On reaching another signpost, follow the path left over a wood plank bridge and through a rather heavy wooden gate. Ignore the stile and signpost on your immediate right and go straight ahead towards the farm buildings. As you walk directly towards the South Downs, you can see on the skyline the circular group of trees known as Chanctonbury Ring. These beech trees were planted in 1760 by a boy called Charles Goring and legend has it that he carried water up the hill for these seedlings until they were sufficiently well established to be able to fend for themselves.

Having walked the length of this rather elongated field, go through a metal gate passing on your left a strangely shaped farmhouse that looks as if it is about to topple over onto one side. Continue through a wooden gate and follow the path through a short stretch of wood ignoring the signposted footpath right. You emerge from the wood and keep straight on for about ¾ mile through a pleasant avenue of trees with woods and fields on either side.

When you eventually come to a made-up road, keep straight on, (i.e. right) and where after a few yards it bends sharp right, keep straight on again along a concrete farm road, as directed by the bridleway sign. You will soon pass on your left a quaint part-wood part-brick cottage with an old-fashioned well in the garden. Don't be tempted to explore, the cottage may look quiet—but there are people in residence. Still following the concrete road, you can at last appreciate the full vista of the South Downs acting as a backcloth to the surrounding countryside and farm ahead.

Well before you reach the farm, there is another bridleway sign directing you off the road and across the fields to your left. Here it is necessary to pass through a barbed wire gate with an intricate fastening! First untwist all the wires holding the gate to the post then slip the pole out of the bottom loop of wire.

Pull down on the pole to remove it from the top loop and you will be able to pass through. You must then reverse the procedure to secure the gate as you found it. Now in the field, turn right and there is another of these wire gates to the right of the drinking trough. However there is plenty of slack in the wire and you should be able to pass between the strands without too much trouble.

Now go straight ahead, keeping the farm buildings to your right and pass through a wide gap in the fence. Cross this field diagonally left to the opposite corner where you will find another bridleway sign by another wire gate. Pass through this gate and another opposite across the farm track. Follow the path through the bushes into the wood where rabbits abound. When you reach a metal gate, do NOT pass through but turn left into a field. Follow the right-hand edge of the field, soon turning right, then left, then right and left again. About 15 yards further on turn right over a wooden pyramid stile to follow a path in the wood. After about 20 yards turn left along a clear joining path. This eventually turns sharp right and leads you to a crossroads where you turn left, into an avenue of fir trees.

Follow this avenue through the plantation until you reach a wooden gate giving access to a road where you turn left. Continue along the road for nearly half a mile passing *Doves Farm* left and *Beggars Bush Kennels* right. Keep to this very pleasant stretch of road with unfenced woods on both sides until just after a *Road Bends* traffic sign on your left. Turn right at the bridleway sign onto anothei path through a wood. Keep straight on ignoring a footpath right and when you come to a junction of paths stay with the same direction keeping a rather mucky pool of water on your right. This path takes you another half mile to a red postbox which you can see well before you reach it. Pass the posbox and continue straight on along the road for about 150 yards to your starting point.

WALK 7

FULKING CIRCULAR.

4½ miles.

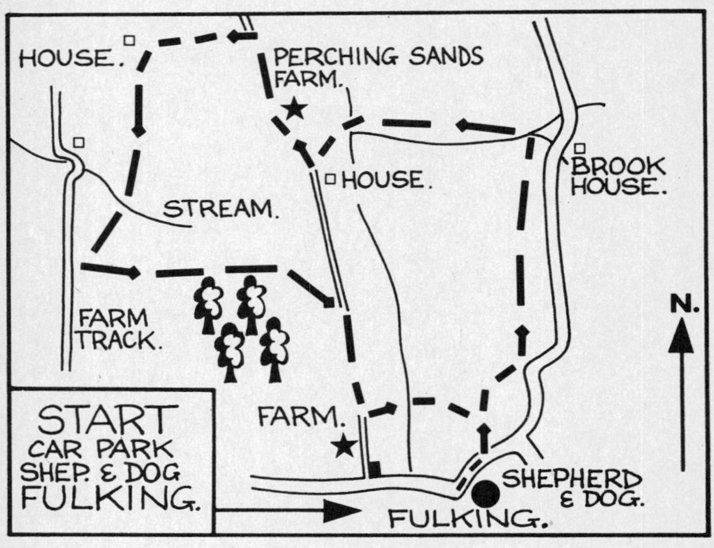

This walk starts and ends at an old coaching inn nestling against the north side of the south downs.

By bus: Southdown Service 106. Tuesdays and Fridays from Brighton—Pool Valley.

By car: A283 from Shoreham. Turn right onto A2037 at Upper Beeding. After about 2 miles, having ascended a long hill and passed a garage on your left, turn right along a minor road to Fulking, which is approximately 2¾ miles further on. The *Shepherd and Dog* is on your right with parking available in the car park or on the verges of the road.

Turn right out of *The Shepherd and Dog* car park, and immediately after passing *Primrose Cottage* on your right, turn left onto a path to the right of a barred gate and to the left of a lovely old thatched cottage. The path leads onto a field with children's swings over to your left and if you turn half right, you will see a footpath sign and stile a few yards ahead. Cross the stile, go down the bank onto a path and turn right. Bear left with the path to the corner of the field and another footpath sign where you go right, through a gap in the fence, and turn left to follow the sign now walking with trees left and open field right.

On coming to another footpath sign by a disused wooden gate, pass to the left of both and carry straight on with the wire fence and hedge left and open field right. There is no obvious path here and you will have to make your way along the narrow strip between the crops and banking. Now is your first chance to look back at the downs. The building on the skyline with a radio mast is the public house at the top of Devils Dyke built on the site of an Iron Age hill fort. As you pass under the pylons you also go through a hedge that is kept cut to keep the footpath open. Immediately cross a wire fence and keep straight on at the left hand edge of the field with a ditch on your left. Cross a farm track and on reaching another footpath sign, go very carefully down the banking to cross a single plank bridge and a stile. Continue straight ahead with a set of three white painted stables on your right. As the hedge breaks away left, you will see a stile in the hedge opposite. Cross the stile, the river, another stile and turn left.

Go straight ahead even though the path appears to bear right and you soon come to a peculiar form of double stile. Negotiate this miniature assault course and follow the direction of the footpath sign as once again there is no visible path. Keep the stream and hedge on your left and having passed under the pylons again, you go through a gap in the hedge which is in fact a bridge over a stream. Go through the gateway and turn left to a 'V' shaped stile in the wire fence ahead. Again keep to the left hand edge of the field following its twists and turns until you finally turn left, passing behind a house, to cross another stile onto a concrete farm road where you turn right.

On reaching the farm, take the left fork and turn left between a farm building right and garden wall left. Turn right with the path and follow this rough wide farm road soon turning left on another concrete road *to Nettledown.* When you reach Nettledown Cottage, keep to the left of the garden entrance and continue along a rough flint-strewn track. At the footpath sign, turn left along the bridleway towards the downs. This path between hedges runs on for half a mile and it has an abundance of wild life which you will see if you walk quietly. Eventually passing through a wooden gate, continue straight ahead. Now, with nothing to block your view, you can appreciate the full panoramic view of the downs spread in front of you.

At the far side of the field, DO NOT turn right as signposted but go straight forward into the next field through a gap in the hedge. (Be prepared to scramble across a ditch). Once in the field, turn half left to cross a wooden sleeper bridge, carefully cross the wire fence and go straight on with fence left and the downs on your right.

Once again there is no visible path and you must make your own way. At the far side of the field, go through the metal gate on your left, turn right over a stile, cross the plank bridge and turn right—that is with the woods on your right. Follow the edge of the field to a metal gate that leads you onto another concrete farm road. Here turn right towards the farm and just before a row of houses, turn left along a wide cart track. Follow this as it bears left then right and when it comes to an end at a metal and wire mesh gate continue straight on with the hedge on your left.

Follow the edge of the field to the corner and the footpath sign. Turn right towards a white painted house and follow the path until you return to the first stile which will be on your left. From here, retrace your steps to the *Shepherd and Dog.*

WALK 8

HICKSTEAD CIRCULAR

4 miles.

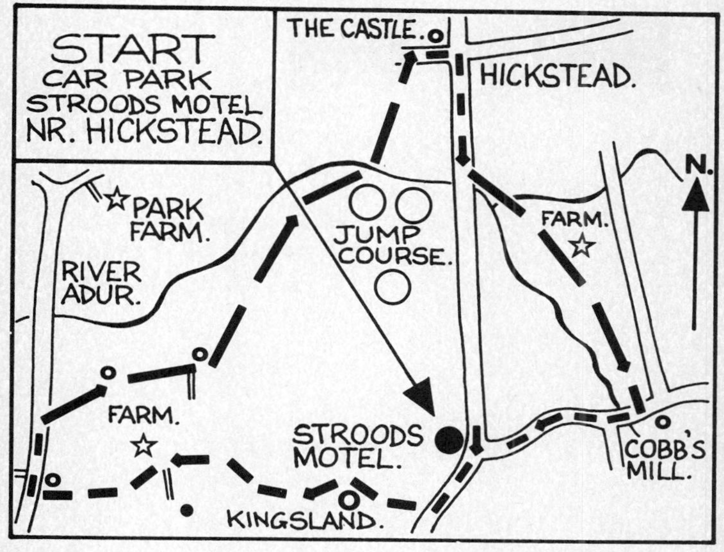

This walk takes you through the country on both sides of the A23 London-Brighton Road just south of Hickstead. Of particular interest is the All-England Jumping Course where you may be lucky enough to see horses and riders in practice.

By car: From North—A23 to Brighton. Having crossed the A272 continue along the A23. Soon after passing *The Castle* public house on your right, you come to *Strood's Motel* also on the right. Turn into the car park. **From South**—The motel is approximately 11 miles from Brighton following the A23. Look out for *Strood's Motel* on your left.

Leave the car park and turn right walking south along the verge of the A23. Turn right through two white gates marked *Kingsland* and go straight ahead along the rough road.

On reaching the entrance to *Kingsland,* bear right, then left, following this now grassy track as it merges with the path from the gardens of *Kingsland.* Continue through a five-barred gate and on along the left hand edge of a field soon having to twist right then left between two ponds. As you walk along the stony cart track you may get an occasional glimpse of the South Downs to your left.

When the cart track joins a concrete road, keep straight on towards the farm buildings. Follow the road past the buildings bearing right then straight ahead towards a house. At the end, the concrete road branches left to avoid a green painted cottage. Although there is a right of way through the cottage garden, it is much easier for you to branch left as well and emerge into a made-up road where you turn right.

You soon come to another concrete road on your right signposted as a public bridleway. Make your way through the farmyard and passing *Petwood Cottage* on the right continue along the stony path. To your left you have views across the comparatively flat mid-Sussex farm country. Ignore a road coming in from the right and go on past *Longhovel Cottage* left. Just after passing some buildings left, and before you go through a gateway where the concrete road ends, strike off left keeping to the right hand edge of the field.

At the corner of the field go over the wooden crossing point and continue to the next corner where you turn right by passing under the single horizontal bar across the gateway. (Be careful of the ditch). Go straight ahead, soon passing through a barred gate. Keep to the left edge of the field, turn left through an entrance to the jumping course and then turn immediately right with the white paling fence on your left. At the corner of the fence by a flag pole turn left and make your way between the various jump areas and jump materials.

You will eventually come to a concrete road where you ignore the turning right leading to a large green building with the sign *Press Office* on the wall, and instead go slightly downhill to cross the bridge over a sluggish river. Go through a small wooden gate and follow the road to a kind of 'T' junction, where you turn right passing stables on your right. Pass through double wooden gates, bear left, then right, and at another 'T' junction turn left following the rough road to a made-up road. Here turn right and a few yards will take you to the A23 at Hickstead crossroads with *The Castle* public house on your left.

In following the next set of directions, it will be necessary to cross the A23. This is an extremely busy arterial road and there is NO pedestrian crossing. Patience is required to wait for a break in the traffic. You may wish to cross at the point suggested, or you may prefer to cross at the crossroads and follow the directions from there. Either way — **extreme care is necessary.**

To continue—Turn right along the A23, and after 90 yards or so, you come to the entrance to *Hickstead Place.* Here cross the road (WITH CARE!) to the wooden footpath sign but **do not go through the hedge.** Instead, continue walking south along the verge of the A23 until the hedge of trees breaks away left. At this point you should see a concrete footpath sign amongst the grass. At certain times this sign becomes overgrown, so watch out for it. Turn left down the banking, over a homemade stile and then cross the field half right to a 'V' shaped stile. (This may also be a little difficult to find so keep a careful lookout). Cross the stile onto a double plank bridge and turn right keeping close to the bank of the stream.

On the far side of the field go through a metal gate with a footpath sign into another field shaped like a dog's leg. Follow the worn path with the stream still on your right. After a 100 yards or so, on your left at the angle of the dog's leg, you will see a wooden gate with another footpath sign. Go through the gate and then immediately right through another gate to follow the righthand edge of the field to a stile in the far corner.

Cross the stile into a road opposite a sign *Cobb's Mill* and turn right passing a charming old cottage called *The Thatch.* Ignore a road left and keep straight on until you once again reach the A23 at *Strood's Motel.* CROSS THE ROAD WITH CARE.

WALK 9

SHIPLEY CIRCULAR

5 miles.

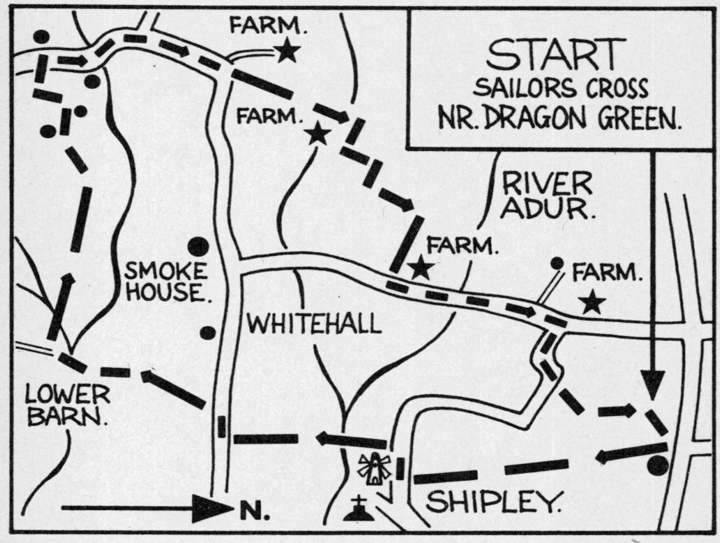

This walk passes through Shipley and visits the house called *Kings Land* where Hilaire Belloc lived from 1906 until his death in 1953. He had his own windmill in the garden and if you get your timing right you can combine the walk with a visit to the mill.

By car: The A272 joins the A29 and A24. From either road, travel along the A272 until you see a sign pointing to *Dragons Green.* Park on the grass verge opposite the sign near a cottage called *Sailors Cross.*

With your back to the road, cross the stile to the right of the cottage garage and follow the direction indicated by footpath sign. There is no visible path but keep to the left edge of the field. As you top the rise, on a clear day, you can see a clump of trees on the downs in the distance. This is Chanctonbury Ring (see Walk No. 6). At the far side of the field, pass through wooden gates, cross the next field, through more gates, and continue along a farm track to a third set of gates and on towards the farm buildings. Over to your left you can see Shipley Church which was built in the 12th century. (This is well worth a visit if you feel like a slight detour).

On reaching the entrance to the farm buildings, turn left along the concrete path for a few yards and then half right, passing a pond right, to a stile in the corner of the field. Keep to the left edge of the field heading towards the house *Kings Land* and the windmill. Cross a stile into the road where you turn right, turning left almost immediately along a tarmacadam road marked as a public bridleway. The road bears left and finishes at the entrance to the mill. It is open to the public between May and October and visitors will normally be given a complete tour on the first Saturday and Sunday of each month between 2.30 and 5.45 p.m.

Turn right along the bridleway with the mill on your left. Cross the bridge over a river and follow the path for some distance to a road. Turn right in the road, turning left after 40 yards or so onto another bridleway. This goes on for half a mile before ending at a five barred wooden gate. Pass through the gate and after a short distance, turn right along the footpath as indicated. Keep heading in this direction even though the path twists round to cross a small brick bridge over a gully.

Keeping to the right edge of the fields, pass through three gates. After the third, turn half left across the field towards the buildings. On the far side, go through another gate to walk along an overgrown path between fences passing a private tennis court left. Go past the single wooden beam onto the gravel drive of the house and follow it as it bends left then right to a road. Turn right and follow the road past some very attractive houses. When the road is joined by another, carry straight on towards *Shipley* and *Dial Post*.

When the road bends sharp right, take the bridleway to the right of a sign for Brooklands farm and Juniper farm. The path goes through a short stretch of wood, and having emerged by way of a small wooden gate, continue ahead towards a black painted farm building. The path passes to the left of this and you immediately turn right between the buildings to the metal gates and a concrete road. Follow the road past the farmhouse and the pond to turn left past the end of the pond and over a twin-barred wooden fence by a metal gate.

Cross the field keeping to the right hand edge and in the far corner, go through a metal gate to turn right along the worn track.

Having passed through *two* more gates, turn left keeping the wire fence on your left. At the far side of the field there is no stile and you must make your own way under the wire fence. Fortunately this is not difficult and having attained the cart track, turn right to the road, then turn left. Keep to the road for half a mile, crossing a river and when you reach a road junction, turn right to *Shipley*.

Keep left using the path on the banking above the road. When this drops to road level, turn left keeping to the road for a short distance before turning left again along the signposted bridleway. Keep to this path between the trees ignoring any stiles on your left. After nearly half a mile it bends right for forty yards, then left, and you soon emerge at your starting point.

WALK 10

ROBERTSBRIDGE (1)

4 miles.

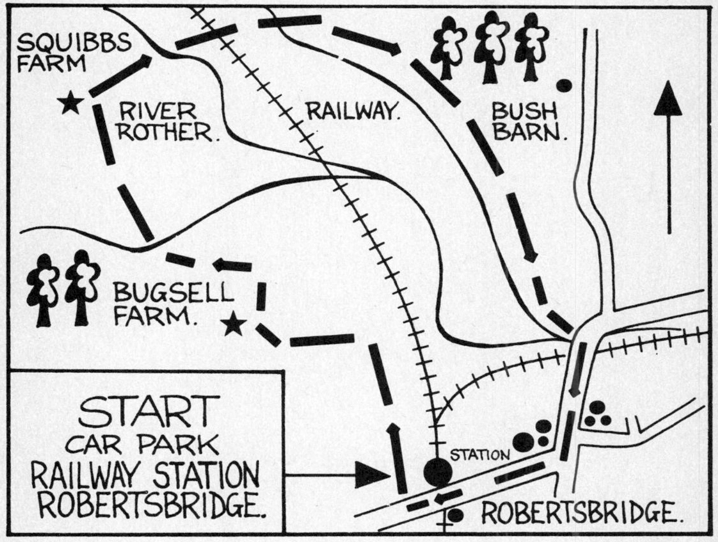

This circular from Robertsbridge gives you an opportunity to combine an easy walk with viewing this attractive little town which grew as an adjunct to an Abbey. (Ruins of the Abbey can be seen during walk 11). *The George* at Robertsbridge is where Hilaire Belloc spent the eve of his walk through Sussex in 1902.

By car: Robertsbridge is on the A21 Hastings road about 5 miles north of Battle. Travelling from the north, you enter Robertsbridge and then turn right at a road with Barclays Bank on the corner, sign posted *Railway Station, Brightling & Dallington.* When you reach the station, turn right into the car park opposite *The Ostrich* public house. If travelling from the south, enter Robertsbridge and just after passing a war memorial in the shape of a clocktower on your left, turn left to the railway station.

Outside the station car park, turn right over the level crossing and turn right again just after the Stores to follow a concrete footpath sign. Go through a metal gate and keep to the righthand edge of the field walking parallel with the railway line on your right.

Go through a gateway with a broken stile then **do not** follow the worn path bearing away left, but keep to the fence on your right, and in the corner of the field, carefully cross a very rickety stile. Keep your direction to another stile and then turn left along a rough farm track. When the track forks, just after emerging between wire fences, take the right-hand minor path leading uphill towards a house.

At the top of the hill, facing the house, turn right following the fence round to the left and in the corner of the field go right through a wooden gate into another field where you turn left. Keep to the left edge of the field, crossing a kind of stile in the corner and follow the green public footpath sign downhill through an avenue of trees. At the bottom of the hill, cross a single plank bridge and a fence. Make your way to the top of the rise and then turn half left downhill to a stone bridge. In the next field, keep left to the corner and cross the fence onto a makeshift bridge of two tree trunks side by side. The best method is a foot on each tree trunk and shuffle!

Safely on the other side, turn left and bear right with the path ignoring a wooden gate left. Pass through the gap in an avenue of trees and continue to where the fence breaks away left. Here turn half left slightly uphill towards the farm buildings and having reached them, turn right and follow the path down to yet another bridge; (a nice solid one this time).

Cross the bridge and with the river on your immediate right, follow the bend to a very solid stile and a railway pedestrian crossing point. Having crossed the line and a second stile, walk straight ahead to the trees opposite and turn right with the trees and river on your left.

For the next mile, continue along this path passing through **FIVE** gates. At the next fence there is no gate, only a stile. When you cross this, you will be walking along a narrow strip of overgrown path with the river left and trees right. If you watch where you put your feet, and keep over to the right, you make safe but slightly uncomfortable progress to a stone bridge and a metal gate. These lead you out into a courtyard surrounded by factory buildings. If however, you find a way over the fence to the right of the stile you can walk quite easily along the edge of a field to pass through a gateway into the factory courtyard.

Make your way across the courtyard following a concrete road with the river on your left past a ruined water mill, to the main road opposite a house called *Salesbury Villa.*

Turn right and follow the road keeping a look out on your left for a bungalow with a fascinating range of old mangles, iron fire grates, and garden ornaments. You are now walking back through Robertsbridge with its old houses before turning right at Barclays Bank to the railway station and your car.

WALK 11

ROBERTSBRIDGE CIRCULAR (2)

4½ miles.

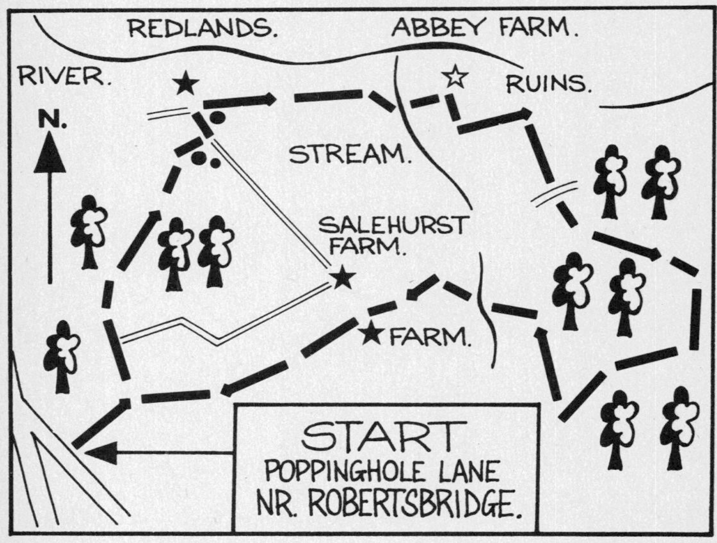

The start is a mile south of Robertsbridge and there is a mixture of woods and rolling farm land giving some marvellous views. You are also able to see the remains of the Cistercian Abbey built about 1190 A.D.

By car: If travelling **from the North,** pass through Robertsbridge on the A21 Hastings road and pass a turning right—to Etchingham. A little further on, turn left into Poppinghole Lane. Go past *Well House* left and nearly opposite a gravel road right you will see a footpath to the left between hedges. Limited parking on grass verges. If you are driving **from the South** along the A21, pass the B2089 right then the A2100 left. Pass the Shell garage *Battle Road Service*

Station left and just after some red and white posts left, turn right into Poppinghole Lane. Then follow instructions as given above.

The footpath starts between hedges, but soon changes to a broad track leading through a wood. Ignore a short crossing track between fields but use the gap in the trees right for a view across the valley.

Continue along the track until you come to a fork where you turn left. You now have the wood on your right and fields left. When the path soon turns sharp right to follow the edge of the wood, you turn left up a short rise and then turn right along the footpath left by the farmer across the middle of the field. You now have another view to your right with the white walls and red roof of Salehurst Farm prominent in the foreground below you. When you reach the corner of a wood, continue in the same direction for about twelve yards and then turn right entering the wood as you do so to follow a clear track.

When you reach a small clearing with a crossing track, keep straight on along the path and downhill until you emerge from the wood at a kind of 'T' junction facing a fenced area with a wooden hut to the left. Here turn left, ducking between two horizontal poles that act as a gate, and follow the path for a short distance bearing slightly right before passing through the twin of the previous gate. Turn right and after a few yards, pass through a wooden gate onto a concrete road.

Follow the road past cottages left to turn left at a 'T' junction. When you reach the farm buildings at another 'T' junction, turn right along the road and follow this for ¾ mile.

The church that dominates the view to your left is Salel Church which was built in the 13th century. At the end of th. straight stretch of road, just after passing a magnificent row of tall poplars, you come to the beautiful old Abbey Farmhouse with what is left of the abbey in part of the garden.

With your back to the farmhouse, pass through a small wooden gate to the right of a large metal gate. Follow the cinder track when it bends left and then right to continue as a concrete road passing (at the time of writing) two unoccupied cottages. A little further on, when the road bends left, go straight ahead along a bridlepath into a wood.

The path makes its way through the wood and there are no

views. Eventually it bears left and climbs fairly sharply uphill and you find at the top that you now have a view across the country to the North-East. You may even be able to pick out Bodiam Castle.

With the view behind you, the path bears right between plantations of fir trees. After about 45 yards, the path bends left but you turn sharp right along a narrow sandy track. To your left and right you see immaculate straight rows of Fir trees. The paths soon broadens and drops downhill to a crossing track at a kind of 'T' junction. Here turn left and follow the path as it also wends an erractic course downhill before bearing right to another crossing track with deep tractor wheel ruts. Cross this (a matter of two or three yards) into an open field and turn left. You soon come to a farm road and you carry straight on towards the farm buildings passing a corrugated iron barn left. To the right across the fields, you can see Salehurst Church again.

When you meet another road, turn left soon passing *Lordship Cottage*. At the point where the road turns sharp left, go ahead through two white painted posts to the right of *Stone Cottage* and to the left of the garage, cross the strip of grass and into a field. Follow the path with trees left and open field right and when the trees break away left, continue along the broad path left between the crops.

You are now walking over an area of farmland. When the path ends in a corner of the field, turn right into a wood and a few yards will bring you to a broad track where you turn left. Keep straight on ignoring a path coming in from the right and you will soon recognise that this path will lead you back to your car.

WALK 12

PLUMPTON CIRCULAR

4 miles.

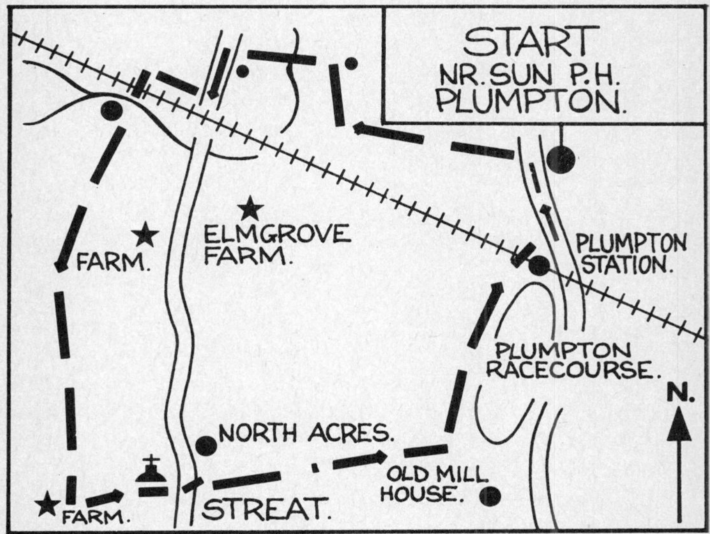

This walk takes you through the secluded hamlet of Streat which lies a little south of the course of an old Roman road called the Greensand Way. As the last ¾ mile is along the outside of the race course, it must be your decision as to whether you choose to spend a day at the races!

By car: Take A275 travelling north from LEWES. Turn left onto the B2116 for just over 2 miles and in Plumpton village (just before the Half Moon public house, turn right for Plumpton race course signposted Plumpton Green. Cross the level crossing and park in the vicinity of *The Sun* public house.

By rail: To Plumpton Station. From the level crossing, turn left for *The Sun* public house.

If you are standing in the road facing *The Sun,* turn left and take the first turning left called *Riddens Lane.* Follow this to a stile to the right of a metal gate and continue along the rough road to a kind of 'T' junction. Cross the stile opposite and make your way to the right hand corner of the field where you pass through a gap in the hedge to follow a worn footpath. You now have a view of the South Downs and the highest 'hump' is in fact Ditchling Beacon.

About two thirds of the way across the field, turn right through a gap in the hedge and then immediately left to another gap, and on along the worn track to a third opening marked by two stout wooden posts. Turn right along this broad bridle path to a metal gate and having passed through, turn left through a gateway to follow twin concrete strips across the field.

On the far side, go through the white painted gate and continue between hedges to emerge from the entrance to *Shergolds Farm.* Turn left in the road and admire the old cottage on your left called *Stonehealed.*

Just before you reach the railway bridge, turn right along a rough track to *Meadowsweet Cottage.* The track is a right of way and you press on between fences to turn left at the end under another railway bridge.

After a few yards, opposite the entrance to a private garden, branch left under the trees to cross a river by the stones provided. Continue ahead passing the house on your right to go through a wooden gate and across the field keeping to the left edge. At the far side, go through a metal gate and straight on towards Ditchling Beacon in the distance. Keep heading towards the Downs passing through two wooden gates and then a metal gate to the left of a house. Carry on along the farm track and you now have a really tremendous view of the Downs. If it is a clear day, look to your right and you can just see the two windmills called the *Jack and Jill* on the skyline above Clayton.

Keep going on this long path through another metal gate and on towards some houses. After passing the first pair of houses, you approach an old beamed farmhouse. On reaching it, turn sharp left along the flint track opposite the front door and less than a ¼ mile will bring you to Streat Place and the church.

Follow the track round to the left and in the road turn left towards a *double bend* road sign. Just before this sign, turn right along another stony road passing an old thatched barn on your left. Keep straight on, passing several houses on both sides of the road with their superb views across the valley to the Downs.

As you progress along the road you will find that you can see across the fields to your left and you may be able to spot a white painted windmill about 4 miles away. You are now walking parallel to a Roman road which passed a little to the north of Streat Church. In fact, the course of the Roman road joins the one on which you are walking just before you reach some more houses.

Having passed these houses and some farm buildings, the rough road becomes smooth and a few yards further on you turn left along a concrete road to the entrance of the racecourse.

Go straight on and when you come to a fork in the road, keep right past the Stable Office right. Keep to this road which passes behind the Grandstand, and when the asphalt path ends, continue ahead keeping the racecourse boundary fence on your immediate right.

Eventually, you must cross the railway footbridge and follow the path to a road where you turn right. At the 'T' junction opposite the school, turn left and you have only a short distance to go before reaching the starting point.

WALK 13

MAYFIELD CIRCULAR

3 miles.

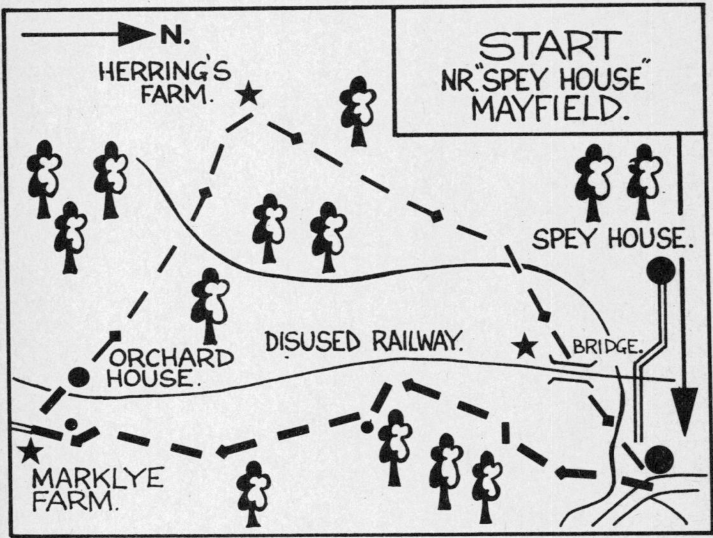

This pleasant walk over a mixed terrain of woods and farmland provides some excellent views across the Rother Valley just south of Mayfield. Mayfield itself is 7 miles south of Tunbridge Wells.

By car: From Tunbridge Wells take the A267 south through Mayfield. Continue past the A272 right and the B2102 right and when the road forks, take the A265 to Heathfield then see below; **From Eastbourne**—A22 north passing A27 left then right. Past A295 right and on reaching a roundabout with A22 left, A271 right, go straight ahead along the A267. After about 7 miles turn right on A265 to Heathfield, then see below:

Pass through Heathfield and just after passing B2203 right, turn left at a small white signpost indicating Mayfield 4 miles.

Keep to the road for 2 miles through a long left bend and then fairly steeply downhill to an old farmhouse on a right bend. This is easily spotted as it has four red, white and black posts on the grass verge in front of it. A little further on past these you will find ample parking on the left verge. DO NOT park on the verge where the posts are:

Having parked your car, make your way back past the house and the bridlepath with the sign *To Spey House and Lodge* and go on a few yards to another Bridleway where you turn right through a metal gate. Follow the worn track over the grass to pass through another metal gate continuing along the path between fences. The path bears right twice, the second time to enter a wood. When you come to a crossing track giving you the option of going on through the wood or turning left—go left. Follow a rather indistinct path at the edge of the wood on your right and when you reach a house, turn right to link with a path leading into the wood again.

Turn left along this FP, passing to the right of the house, and the bushes soon open out to leave a clear, well-used track. Keep going for ½ mile passing under some pylons stretching across the countryside, and eventually you leave the wooded area and continue along a stony road between hedges.

You are now able to see a panoramic view across the valley through gaps in the hedge. At the top of the rise pass a house and barn right and you can see *Marklye Farm* ahead. Just before you reach the farm, turn right along a tarmac road to Orchard House. As the road takes you downhill, you get another view across the Rother Valley and to your right is the built up area of Mayfield. The road and right of way take you through a white painted barrier and on across the frontage of Orchard House to a metal gate. Go through the gate and down the centre of the field to cross a stile at the bottom.

Make your way across the stream, up the opposite bank and through a gap in the fence to follow the FP through the wood. Go straight across the wide crossing track and on along the narrow but well defined path. This soon drops downhill and you must cross another stream by a single plank bridge. Leaving the wood behind you, go straight on uphill to the farm ahead. At the top of the hill, if you look back, you can see *Orchard House* across the valley.

Keep to the right of the farm buildings, turn right and ignoring a metal gate left, go straight on through a gap in the wooden fence. Follow this broad grassy path between hedges to a metal gate and on the other side keep to the path as it goes downhill between earth banks.

Pass under the pylons again and when the worn path turns left into a field, you go straight on under the trees between the banking. A short distance takes you to a wooden bridge crossing a river, and the path continues on the other side through an avenue of trees to a rough wooden gate. The clear track runs ahead and then bears right uphill to farm buildings. Instead of going straight on through the buildings, take the turning left and the last building on your right is a brick built bungalow called *Stella.* The rough road bears gently right under a railway bridge and on to a made up road where you turn right. A short distance brings you to the road where you left your car.

WALK 14

BATTLE (NO. 1).
3 miles.

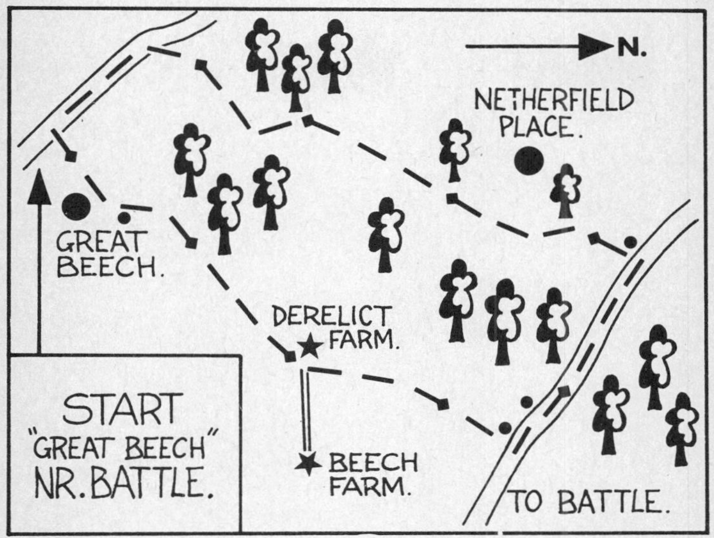

For the most part you will be walking through woods and there are numerous picnic spots, particularly on the return journey through Ashes Wood. I recommend this walk for any time of the year but during blackberry time, you have a bonus. Blackberry bushes abound en route so be sure to take large baskets or polythene bags because, away from the roads, the blackberries are huge.

By car: From Battle take the A269 travelling West and in just over a mile, turn right onto the B2096. About 350 yards on, stop at the entrance to *Great Beech* on your right. It is easily recognisable from the small grass triangle and white painted stones in front of the gate and you have the almost hidden entrance to *Crelancot* to its left. If you can park here safely without blocking either entrance do so, but you would be well advised to go on a little further and turn right into the entrance of another footpath and walk back.

Go through the gate to *Great Beech* and after a short distance along this rough road you come to the house. This is an attractive old building with a well maintained garden and its own oast house. Continue along the road that gradually becomes a stony track through an avenue of trees, and your blackberry gathering can start now. (Do not linger too long, the bigger ones are farther on). After a while, derelict farm buildings come into view ahead and you make straight for these ignoring a path into the wood on your right. The path to the farm is blocked by two or three pieces of wooden fence tied together but these may be untied to proceed along the right of way.

The actual right of way through the buildings has also been blocked off and so a slight detour must be made. When you come to a dead-end facing the open side of a corrugated roofed barn, turn left to the brick building. (The right of way goes between these two buildings and should be taken if ever the blockage is removed). At the corner of the brick cowshed, side step left then continue forward up a bank under the trees. You must now turn right crossing the two low stone walls of an outbuilding and turn right again to reach the back of the corrugated roofed barn. From here the right of way goes up between the fence left and the farmhouse right to the bridle path which has been fenced off and is now overgrown.

However, all is not lost, we shall go another way and reach the largest blackberries at the same time.

At the barn, turn left keeping the fence (and the farmhouse) on your right. This takes you uphill through a gap in the hedge and you are now walking with open field left and the wood and bridle path right. Keep straight on with the fence on your right and it is along here that you should find those nice big juicy blackberries! If you look back, you have a fine view across the woods to *Great Beech.*

Press on uphill, through another gap in a hedge and as you near the top corner of the field, you will see there is no way out.

Therefore, about 25 yards before the corner, at a point where a tree on the other side of the fence bends away from you, carefully pass between the slack fence wires to regain the bridle path.

Turn left along the path which is not so overgrown now and follow this well defined way through the wood for nearly ½ mile. At the end of the path, make your way over the broken gate and the rough stile immediately opposite into a road where you turn left.

Just after passing Fir Tree Cottage left, make a point of finding a gap in the hedge on your right to see the view. Keep going along this quiet road with woods on either side until you come to a small red post box fixed to a telegraph pole. Turn left immediately before this, passing the gate to *Ashes Lodge* on your right. When, after a few yards, the road bears right, branch left to follow a footpath with fence right and wood left. Go through a wooden gate, the entrance to Ashes Wood, and keep straight on along the broad path ignoring a wider path that sweeps off left. After ¾ mile you cross a brick walled bridge and when after a few yards the paths fork, turn left.

The path makes a gradual bend right and where it straightens out, ignore another path leading off right and go ahead. You soon pass through another wooden gate, thus leaving the Forestry Commission area and a 100 yards or so will bring you out to a road.

You have emerged from the entrance to the footpath suggested as a secondary parking area at the beginning of the walk. If you parked your car here the walk is finished, if not, turn left in the road and a short distance will bring you back to the entrance of *Great Beech*.

WALK 15

BATTLE (NO. 2)

3½ miles.

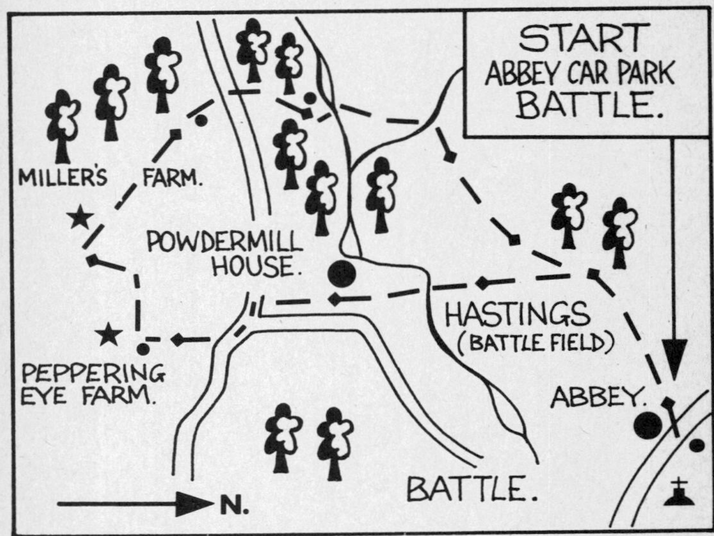

Starting at Battle Abbey, you walk through the scene of the Battle of Hastings, 1066, and return past a secluded lake. The Abbey is well worth visiting as is the museum opposite.

By car: From any direction to Battle Abbey Car Park.

By bus: Routes 252 and 253 from Hastings or Tunbridge Wells to the Maidstone & District office in Battle. Then make your way to the Abbey.

From the Abbey car park facing the entrance to the Abbey, turn right passing the *Pilgrims restaurant* on your right. Follow the stony path through a wooden gate to the left of a metal gate now walking with a wood left and open field right. Go on through another wooden gate and on along a well-worn path.

When the wood breaks away left at a fork in the path, take the left fork.

You are now walking through the fringe of the battlefields, most of the battle having taken place in the grounds to your left. At the bottom of the hill, pass through a metal gate and continue ahead with hedge left and open field right. When the hedge breaks away left, cut across the middle of the field to a stile. Cross the stony track that leads to *Powdermill House* (see Museum) and enter the field opposite.

Make your way to the far side, a distance of about 8 yards and turn right now walking downhill parallel to a road behind the hedge on your left. At the bottom of the field, drop down through a gap in the hedge and turn left to a road. Cross this road to a minor road (signposted *Crowhurst*) and follow it for a short distance before turning right to *Peppering Eye Farm* (see Museum).

Just before the farm and just after *Stone Cottage* turn right over the fence with its remains of a stile by a gate. The FP now takes you along a grassy bank with fence and trees left and open field down to your right. On the far side, go through a wooden gate into another field and keep to the left hand edge until you reach a stile. Once over the stile, carefully pass between the slack wires of a fence, and turn right to the top corner of the field where you then turn left towards the farm buildings.

When you reach the concrete farm road, turn right. This soon bends right and continues as twin concrete strips for nearly ½ mile. Eventually you come to a road which you cross slightly right to a stile and follow the well defined path through the wood. After a while, the path descends fairly sharply to a quiet lake where you cross the stream by a single plank bridge.

Continue along the path as it bends right and climb gradually until you emerge from the wood at a broken stile. Cross the field half-right to another stile giving you access to a bridleway between fences where you turn right, almost immediately crossing a third stile by a metal gate. Continue along the bridleway for a ¼ mile to yet another stile and then follow the worn path as it bears left and uphill through the gorse. At the top of the hill your path is joined by one leading in from the right which is in fact the outgoing path when you took the left fork.

From this point, you retrace your steps keeping the wood on your right and after passing through two wooden gates you will find yourself back at Battle Abbey.

WALK 16

CRAWLEY CIRCULAR.

5½ miles.

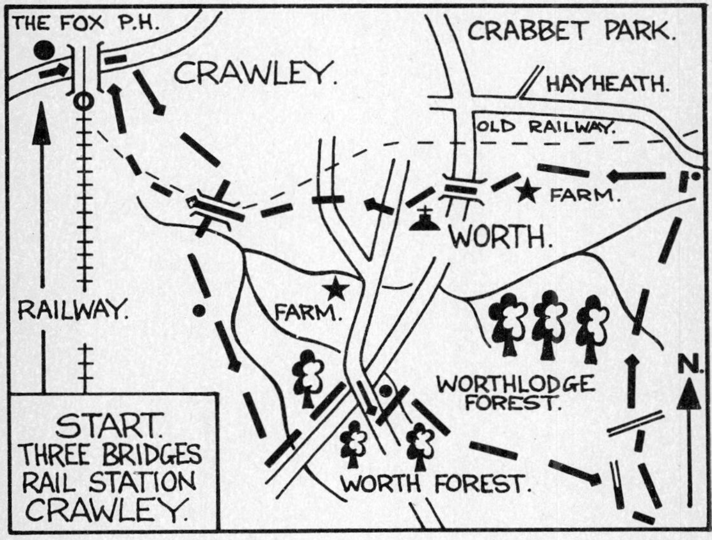

This walk takes you through Worth Forest just a 'stone's throw to the south-east of Crawley and returns via the old Saxon church at Worth.

By car: To Three Bridges Railway Station and park as close as possible.

By train: To Three Bridges Station.

With your back to the Three Bridges Railway Station and facing the *Fox* public house, turn right under the bridge and then first right into a wide road. You soon come to the entrance of *Hellermann Cassettes Limited,* where you go straight on along a narrow footpath between wire fences leaving the road on your right. When the path opens out into a playing field, keep to the right hand edge of the field and on the far side, once again continue along a narrow path with allotments left until you go down some wooden steps into a narrow lane. Here turn right under a small metal bridge and ignoring tracks left and right, go straight ahead with fence left and stream right. Go over the bridge and straight on between the trees to a grassy track with fields on either side. (If the ground is really muddy, climb up on the bank to your right).

On reaching a solitary house, keep it to your right and go straight on. Where the path opens out, bear left along a clear track, crossing yet another stream by way of a bridge made of sleepers, to a rather uninviting gate wrapped round with barbed wire. Go through the gate and then ahead following the path through the centre of the field to the trees on the far side, ignoring a track leading off to the left. Here, at a kind of 'T' junction, turn left and to your right you become conscious of the sound of speeding cars. This is explained when the path opens out and you find yourself walking above and parallel to the M23.

On reaching the bridge, turn right (crossing the M23) and cross the road to the left hand side, where at a small white garden gate bearing the name *Cuffs* you turn left. DO NOT take the track leading up through the trees on your right, but carry straight on keeping to the left of the pylons. The path bears left over a river and where it forks, keep right with the Fire Hazard sign left. You now stay on this path for about a mile. Climb steadily uphill ignoring tracks left and right and carry straight on eventually passing a public footpath sign on your right. You are now walking through a part of Worth Forest and the fir trees stand tall and straight around you. When you reach a type of crossroads, keep straight on as directed by a second footpath sign and still ignoring any 'offshoots' you eventually come to a 'T' junction opposite a '*Riding by Permit Only*' sign where you turn right.

Keep to this sandy track as it bears left and when it meets a reddish coloured road, turn left almost doubling back on yourself. When the red sandy path ends, continue ahead along the stony road ignoring tracks left and right. The road goes on through the wood for ¾ mile ending at a white gate. DO

NOT go through the gate, but branch left along a worn path for about 12 yards to a bridleway and FP signpost. Drop down through a gap in the fence and turn left along the bridleway. Follow this for half a mile to a road with farm buildings left.

Cross the road to the continuation of the bridleway and through a novel form of chain gate. Follow the bridlepath through a gateway and then across a bridge over the M23. An uphill track takes you to Worth Church. This 10th-century church is considered to be the finest Saxon Church in Sussex and a visit is recommended. At the top of the hill, you find a kind of 'T' junction, turn left for Worth Church or right to continue the walk. After a short distance, cross a road and keeping to the right of a house called *The Buttfield,* continue along a track between gardens. On reaching another road, cross both the road and stile to follow the footpath through the middle of a field to another stile. Go over this and a single tree trunk bridge over a stream, then uphill to a crossing track. At this point go neither right nor left but ahead over the bank dropping down onto the disused railway line, now a footpath, where you turn left.

Eventually you cross a small metal bridge and farther on, just as it looks as though you will have to walk along the railway line into Three Bridges Station, opposite the signal box the track turns into a made up road. Follow this down to the main road (A264) and turn left under the railway bridge for Three Bridges Station.

WALK 17

SLAUGHAM.

1¼ miles.

I make no apologies for the fact that this is more of a stroll than a walk. Slaugham is such a delightful little village with its mixed variety of cottages and houses that it has to be included somehow.

By car: From the North—A23 Brighton road changing to the A279 at Handcross. After about 1½ miles, turn left at a cross roads with the 'Wheatsheaf' public house on the corner, signposted *Slaugham 1 mile.* Go straight over the crossroads and continue to Slaugham Church where there is ample parking space. **From the South**—Take the A281 from Henfield (North of Shoreham) and turn right on the A279. Go past the B2115 right and turn right at the crossroads by *The Wheatsheaf* public house. From there follow directions as given above.

From the car park go through the entrance to the church and follow the brick path round to the left until it ends at a wooden door in the side of the church. From here, branch right along the churchyard path passing a big old gnarled tree on your right and when the path ends, continue across the strip of grass to a stile in the fence. In the field, turn half-right towards a house and when you reach the boundary fence, cross another stile into the garden.

Make your way down the garden towards the house, stopping for a moment to look over a gate on your left (*No Admittance*) at the ruins of *Slaugham Place*. Continue, heading for the left hand corner of the house and don't be embarrassed if the family are in the garden. They are quite used to people walking through but understandably they are making application to divert the path away from their garden, so look out for any diversion sign.

At the corner of the house, bear half left to pass a clump of trees, go down a slight bank and follow the trodden path as it bends left towards a bridge. Go over the bridge and onto the road where you turn left. Almost immediately, turn right in another road having passed through a white gate and follow the road past *Slaugham Manor* with its two stone lions. Go on past *Lakeside Cottage* and immediately after passing a barrier marked—*Private Road. Slaugham Place Farm* turn right to follow the path round the lake.

The path bends left through the trees and you should look out for a stone wall on your right. If you look over the wall, you will see that you are standing on top of a stone arch with steps leading down to the water.

A few yards further will take you out of the trees and onto a path where you turn right. You soon come to a stile that leads you between fences to another stile and on through the churchyard back to your car.

This is really the end of the walk, but I suggest that you go on past *The Chequers* to see the houses before returning to that pleasant inn for refreshment.

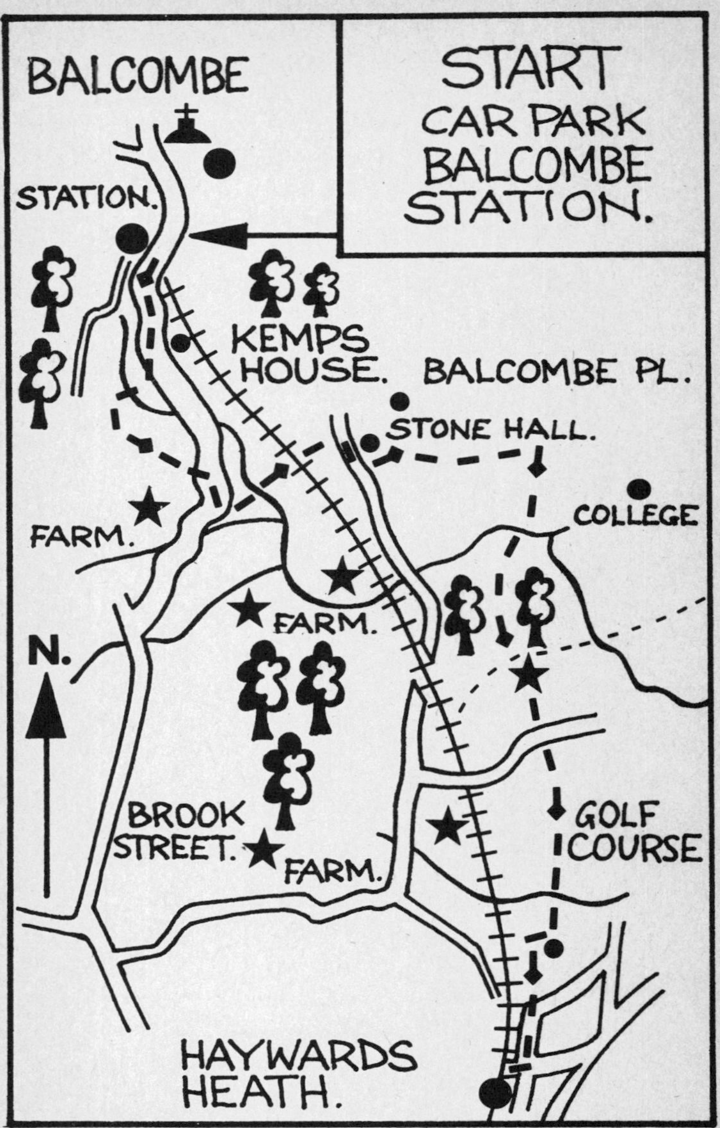
BALCOMBE
START
CAR PARK
BALCOMBE
STATION.
STATION.
KEMPS
HOUSE.
BALCOMBE PL.
STONE HALL.
COLLEGE
FARM.
FARM.
N.
BROOK
STREET.
FARM.
GOLF
COURSE
HAYWARDS
HEATH.

WALK 18

BALCOMBE TO HAYWARDS HEATH

5¾ miles.

This is the second A to B walk and I always think of it as the Bluebell Walk because in May the woods are covered with a blue carpet.

At one point for a short distance you follow the route of a Roman road from London to Brighton. However, unlike the Roman soldiers, we are unable to walk the countryside in a straight line and so you soon have to veer away to follow the footpaths of today.

By car or train: To Balcombe station on the London-Brighton line. Return by rail from Haywards Heath station.

Leave Balcombe Station via the car park on the west side. On leaving the entrance to the car park, turn right ignoring the footpath and stile right, and continue along the road until you come to *Kemp's House* left. Go through the gate on your right opposite the house and bear left to another gate in the hedge that leads into a large field. Go diagonally right downhill towards the trees and look for a not very obvious stile. Cross the stile and a single plank bridge over a stream, then follow the path uphill through the trees. When you reach an old wooden shed, bear left up a track opposite the door, and at the top of the short rise where the path forks, take the left-hand lower path.

Continue to follow this broad grassy winding track through the trees where the ground is carpeted with bluebells in May. Eventually, you go downhill to a three-barred gate and the main road. Turn right, walking along the grass verge crossing the road when necessary to continue walking on grass. Pass a *Sharp Bend* road sign and on reaching the right-hand bend, turn left over a stile. Keeping close to the hedge on your left, go straight on downhill and soon the path continues between two rows of trees with a wood right. Cross the river by using the one plank bridge, ignore the stile left, and instead, bear half-right to the edge of the wood. Continue by keeping to the left-hand edge of the field until you come to a stile giving access to a railway crossing point. Cross the line into a large field (sometimes ploughed) and turn right. Turn left at the corner of the field, and follow the line of trees up to another stile. Here the original footpath is blocked by a fence, so having crossed the stile, turn immediately right along a rough tree root-strewn path between fences to follow the diverted right of way.

Follow the left-hand fence bearing left then right to a three-barred wooden gate. Go through the gate onto a concrete path that leads you to the road opposite Stone Hall Farm. Turn right, bear right with the road and turn left through a stone gateway by a gatehouse. Proceed along the made up road and on reaching the cattle grid, turn right along another concrete road. The building you can see on your left now is *Balcombe Place.* Go past an oak-beamed cottage right and at two metal gates, take the left-hand gate and turn right keeping to the right-hand edge of the field. Turn left at the corner of the field and then right through a wooden gate into another field. Go straight ahead (no visible path) keeping the wood on your immediate left and when the wood breaks away left, bear half right across the field to a metal gate in the hedge. Through the gate, half-left across the field and downhill to a stile some 40 yards to the left of three tall silver birch trees.

Go over the stile and down some stone steps to a crossing track where you turn right. This leads downhill through a wooden gate. The bridge you see to your left is on the site of a bridge made by the Romans for the road they built from London through Croydon and Godstone to Brighton. Having come through the wooden gate, turn sharp right uphill through another gate or over a stile and follow the grassy footpath with hedge on your immediate left. You are now walking along what is called the AGER or earthen platform that supported the Roman road. This gives you a good view of *Ardingly College,* a public school, on your left.

At the far corner of the field, bear right (away from the Roman road) and after crossing a double stile left, turn left and make your way down to a bridge. Cross the bridge, bear right to a second bridge and then half-right to a three-barred gate and stile. You are now entering River's Wood, the second point on this walk where bluebells abound.

Continue along a broad track ignoring all crossing tracks until you come to another stile which takes you onto a rough road where you turn left. Carry straight on through the farm buildings, (keeping the old oak-beamed house on your right) to a stile by a metal barred gate. Continue ahead to a double stile crossing a ditch and straight across the field to another stile opposite. Having crossed this stile, be very careful because part of the old wooden bridge is missing.

Keep to the right of the house ahead and over yet another stile to follow the broad grassy track to a fence and road. Go through the gate, cross the road, go over another stile and along the bridle path up through the woods. When you reach a semi-clearing where a lot of trees have been felled and with a large wooden building on the edge of the golf course, **do not** go across the golf course but bear right keeping just inside the edge of the wood with the golf course left. Be careful because the main track turns off right, so be sure to keep to the path with the fence and golf course on your immediate left. Eventually you come to the edge of the wood with a stile leading into a large field. Carry straight on with the golf course still on your left.

At the far side of the field, drop down into a kind of gully, go over another stile and follow the footpath at the bottom of the gully, until you appear to come to a dead end. Here you go through a gap in the bushes on your left and turning right, you continue along the footpath to cross a small wooden bridge before you eventually arrive at a gravel road opposite the gates of a large beamed house. If the gates are open take time to admire the view of the house and the simple but effective layout of the garden.

Turn right along the gravel road, go through a gateway and immediately turn left along Wickham Way. You are now walking along a road with a variety of different houses on both sides. On reaching the main road, turn right then immediately left into Millgreen Road. At the top of the road you come to a busy roundabout and Haywards Heath Station is on your right.